FUNNY SIDE UP

THE EGGSTREMELY

WITTY JOKE BOOK

BY MARK WHITE

WORK & MONEY

The machine at the coin factory suddenly stopped working for no reason.

It doesn't make any cents!

~

I just bought an expensive new car and found out the reverse gear was broken right after I drove out.

There's no going back now.

~

I finally got my dream job as a church bell ringer!

Today's my first day so they're just showing me the ropes.

~

Karate: the ancient Japanese art of getting people to buy lots of belts.

~

I'm looking to hire a group of people to move toxic waste from a nearby nuclear reactor.

I can't pay anyone but I'm sure they'll get plenty of exposure.

~

I don't think I'm strong enough for my job as a personal trainer anymore.

I'll probably have to hand in my too-weak notice.

~

No matter how hard I try and buy supermarket conveyor belt dividers, the cashier always puts them back.

~

I just got fired from my new job at the pharmacy.

Apparently "drug free workplace" and "free drug workplace" are not the same thing at all.

~

What do you call a cheap wig?

A small price toupee.

~

Acupuncture - now that's a jab well done.

~

I was going to tell you some tax jokes...

but I doubt you'd depreciate it.

~

"Are you actually a professional yo-yo player?"

"Nah, it's just a wind-up."

~

I got fired today for leaving unfinished work over the weekend.

What were they thinking? Surgeons are only human.

~

I love my job as a feces inspector...

but my wife hates it when I bring my work home with me.

~

The Chinese government is seizing my land to build a cemetery.

It has to be a Communist plot.

~

A man is walking in a graveyard when he hears the Third Symphony played backward. When it's over, the Second Symphony starts playing, also backward, and then the First. "What's going on?" he asks the cemetery worker.

"It's Beethoven," says the worker, "He's decomposing."

~

Today I gave up my seat to a blind lady on the bus.

And that's how I lost my job as a bus driver.

~

The office Christmas party...

a great opportunity to catch up with people you haven't seen for 20 minutes.

~

I own a second hand DeLorean...

but I only use it from time to time.

~

I still can't believe I got fired from the calendar factory.

All I did was take a day off.

~

How do you land a plane without crashing?

And hurry up; I can already see the runway!

~

How much does a circumciser get paid?

Nothing, he just keeps the tips.

~

"How much wood have you chopped?"

"Not sure, let me check the logs."

~

Sorry for the long wait at the ER.

Thanks for your patients.

~

Someday I'm going to achieve my goal in life and provide everyone with free eye care...

you'll see...you'll all see!

~

I went to see a handwriting expert yesterday.

She could tell I was laid-back, gullible and well-off just from a signature on a cheque.

~

To the guy who stole my Microsoft Office, I will find you. You have my word.

~

Did you hear about the mathematician who's afraid of negative numbers?

He will stop at nothing to avoid them.

~

Can a woman make her husband a millionaire?

Of course, if he's a billionaire.

~

I've been working on my PhD in engineering for the past five years, but my kids don't necessarily see that as work.

As we were driving past Walmart one day, my son spotted a 'Now Hiring' sign and suggested that I could get a job there.

Hoping to make a point, I asked, "Do you think they're looking for an engineer?"

"Oh sure," he said, "They'll hire anybody."

~

I'm a very successful scarecrow which isn't a job for everyone...

but hay, it's in my jeans.

~

I once met an anesthesiologist for a brain surgeon.

She said the pay was great, but the work was mind numbing.

~

Have you heard of the constipated mathematician?

He had to work it out with a pencil.

~

I got fired from my job at the bank today.

Some elderly lady asked me to check her balance.

So I pushed her over.

~

Cop: Whose car is this? What do you do for a living? Where are you going?

Miner: Mine.

~

When I was a train driver a colleague approached me and said, "My boss keeps yelling at me for derailing trains, can you help me?"

I said, "Sure, I can get you back on track."

~

Interviewer: "So what did you learn from your previous job?"

Me: "That I need a new job."

~

For every dollar a man makes, a woman makes 80 cents. That is outrageous!

Why is the man only left with 20 cents?

~

The devil visits a politician and makes him an offer.

"I can arrange some things for you," the devil says, "I can get you billions of dollars, unlimited political influence, and anything else you can dream of. All I ask for in return is death, disease, and poverty for millions of people around the world."

The politician thinks for a moment and says, "What's the catch?"

~

A young man wants to join the Navy. "Can you swim?" the recruiter asks him.

"Why, don't you have boats?"

~

I never wanted to believe that my dad stole from his job as a road worker.

But when I got home, all the signs were there.

~

The village blacksmith hired an enthusiastic new apprentice willing to work long, hard hours. He instructed the boy, "When I take the shoe out of the fire, I'll lay it on the anvil. When I nod my head, you hit it with the hammer."

The apprentice did exactly as he was told, and now he's the new village blacksmith.

~

I told my boss that three companies were after me and I needed a raise.

My boss asked, "What companies?"

"Gas, water and electricity."

~

My first day on the job at an IKEA store, I was told by my boss that employees needed to go to the meeting room before every shift.

I said, "Do I need to?" He said, "Assembly is required."

~

I've always wondered how much a cemetery makes?

It must be a killing.

~

After I took a job at a small publishing house, the first books I was assigned to edit were all on the topic of dieting.

"Isn't the market flooded with these types of books?" I asked another editor, "How can we expect to turn a profit?"

"Don't worry," he assured me, "These books appeal to a wide audience."

~

The gladiator was having a rough day in the arena. His opponent had sliced off both his arms and lopped off both his feet.

The gladiator had been unarmed and defeated.

~

As a doctor, I'm addicted to hitting my patients on their knees to test their reflexes.

I get a real kick out of it.

~

Why are farmers, who take a good inventory of their cows, so efficient at chemical reactions?

They have a cattle list.

~

Two lawyers went into a diner and decided to order drinks.

They felt hungry after a long day so they produced sandwiches from their briefcases and started to eat them.

Frustrated, the owner marched over and told them, "Listen, you're not allowed to eat your own sandwiches in here!"

The lawyers looked at each other, shrugged their shoulders and then exchanged sandwiches.

~

Why was the clock salesman bored?

He had too much time on his hands.

~

If women knew how much money I had, they wouldn't call me ugly.

They'd call me ugly AND poor.

~

My doctor said he's been practicing for 30 years.

When is he going to start doing his job for real?

~

A friend and I used to run a business selling tee-shirts with a big X and sunglasses printed on them. One day I said to my friend, "What's going on, this order was supposed to go out a week ago!"

He said, "I'm nearly done, I've just got to dot the eyes and cross the tees."

~

I was in a cab today and the cab driver said, "I love my job. I'm my own boss and the best part is that nobody tells me what to d..."

"Turn left here."

~

Did you hear about the man who paid to enter a marathon?

They gave him a good run for his money.

~

My girlfriend borrowed $100 from me. After 3 years, when we separated, she returned exactly $100.

I lost Interest in that relationship.

~

What did the ill comedian say at the hospital?

"I'm here...all weak!"

~

Have you heard of the soldier who survived a pepper spray and mustard gas attack?

He's a seasoned veteran.

~

I used to sell security alarms door to door, and I was really good at it.

If no one was home, I would just leave a brochure on the kitchen table.

~

Two carpenters hard at work were talking about their previous jobs.

"I got the sack once for being just two mil out!" the first one said.

"That was a bit unreasonable." replied the second.

"It was alright," said the first one, "I didn't really want to be an accountant anyway."

~

What is an engineer's first job out of high school?

Aquathermic treatment of ceramics, aluminum, and steel.

Or to put it in layman's terms: washing dishes.

~

I wouldn't want to be my own boss...

that guy's an asshole.

~

How did the bag of fertilizer help the vegetable farmer pay his mortgage?

It raised his celery.

~

I used to be a gutter installer but I had to quit as it was too draining.

~

A farmer was picking apples when he heard a noise from his pond. He walks over and sees three young women skinny dipping.

They notice him and crouch in the water up to their shoulders. "Go away! Stop spying on us!"

The farmer says, "Sorry ladies, but I didn't come out here to see you naked," holding up his apple bucket he says, "I came to feed the alligator."

~

People always ask me what it was like running a business with the world's tallest man.

And to them I say, it was good but when it came to making tough decisions, we didn't always see eye to eye.

~

I found a wallet with 20 dollars in it. I wasn't sure what to do but then I thought, "What would Jesus do?"

So I turned it into wine.

~

My boss pulled up to work today in his brand new Lincoln

As he got out of the car, I said to him, "Wow, that's a nice car!"

He notices my admiration and says, "Well, you know what? If you work hard and put in the hours, I'll have an even better one next year."

~

I had a job interview today and I have a feeling it went well. The manager said they were looking for somebody responsible.

"You've found your man," I responded, "Whenever there was a problem in my last job, they always said that I was responsible!"

~

As I get older and remember all the people I've lost along the way, I think to myself...

perhaps I shouldn't have pursued a career as a tour guide...

~ ~ ~

FAMILY & FRIENDS

My friend likes to take the elevator, while I like to take the stairs.

I guess we were raised differently.

~

I asked my daughter if she'd seen my newspaper. She told me that newspapers are old school. She said that people use tablets nowadays and handed me her iPad.

That fly didn't stand a chance.

~

Dad washing car with son

Son: "Dad, can't you just use a sponge?"

~

I was playing chess with my friend, when he said,
"Let's make this more interesting."

So we stopped playing chess.

~

I took my mother-in-law out last night.

I'm loving my new sniper rifle.

~

I was out in the garden with my stepladder today.

Not my real ladder, I don't get along with my real
ladder.

~

I kept meeting my Chinese friend in the elevator
today...

it was Wong on so many levels.

~

I bought a 12 year old scotch the other day.

Her parents weren't too happy.

~

My buddy laughed at me when I told her I could make a car out of spaghetti.

You should've seen the look on her face when I drove pasta!

~

I asked my friend from North Korea what it's like there.

He said, "Can't complain."

~

My mailman friend tells a lot of jokes about undelivered letters.

But no one seems to get them.

~

A friend said that I have the potential to be a really great comedian.

He said I just needed to improve my punchlines.

~

My sister was born without her pinky toe and the sight of her foot makes me physically ill.

My therapist says I'm lack-toes intolerant.

~

I rode the elevator to the eleventh floor and as I got out, the operator said, "Have a good day son."

"Don't call me son," I said, "You're not my dad."

"No, but I brought you up, didn't I?"

~

My grandpa had the heart of a lion...

and a lifetime ban from the local zoo.

~

My friend is struggling to find a job as an optician friend.

I guess good contacts are important.

~

My transgender atheist friend doesn't like to talk about her childhood.

She was a heathen.

~

Why didn't Adam have a mother-in-law?

Because he lived in paradise.

~

Father: "Son, I need to tell you something...you were adopted."

Son: "What I knew it! I want to meet my biological parents!"

Father: "We are your biological parents. Now pack your things, your new parents are picking you up in 20 minutes."

~

My neighbor is in the Guinness Book of Records. He's had 44 concussions. He lives very close to me.

A stone's throw away, in fact.

~

I was driving with my cousin when he blew through a red light.

"Are you crazy?!" I yelled.

He waved me off, saying, "It's OK, my brother does it all the time."

The next light was red too, and he just sailed on through again.

"You're gonna get us killed!" I shouted.

And he again replied, "It's OK, my brother does it all the time."

The next light was green, so I was feeling better, but my cousin slammed on the brakes.

I asked, "Now what?"

He said, "Gotta be careful, my brother might be coming the other way."

~

"Son, what do you want to be when you grow up?"

"A garbage man," he replied.

"That's an unusual one, why's that then?"

"So I only have to work on Tuesdays."

~

I went to school with a blind kid and every time a classmate made a joke the blind kid would laugh.

Confused, I asked my friend how this was possible.

He said, "He's just got a really good sense of humor."

~

A friend asked if the ceiling was my favorite part of my house.

I said, "Not my favorite, but it's up there!"

~

My nine-year-old and I passed a store with a sign that read: "Watch Batteries Installed - $5"

He seemed confused and said: "Who would pay to watch batteries installed?"

~

Why can't a woman ask her brother for help?

Because he can't be a brother and assist her too.

~

Me: "Have you heard of Murphy's Law?"

Friend: "Of course, it's the theory that says anything that can go wrong will go wrong."

Me: "Ok, have you heard of Cole's law?"

Friend: "No, I haven't actually."

Me: "It's thinly-sliced cabbage in mayonnaise."

~

When I was a child my father attacked me with cameras; I still have flashbacks.

~

"Dad, are bugs good to eat?" asked the boy.

"Let's not talk about such things at the dinner table," his father replied.

After dinner, the father inquired, "Now, son, what did you want to ask me?"

"Oh, nothing," the boy said, "There was a bug in your soup, but now it's gone."

~

I love Humpty Dumpty!

He's one shell of a guy!

~

My housemates threw a moving-out party for me.

I just wish they did it before I left.

~

Every night, my roommate gets high and watches the Benjamin Button movie in reverse.

I finally said, "This is getting old really fast."

~

"Mom? Don't freak out, but I'm in the hospital..."

"Steve, you've been a doctor for over 8 years now, please stop starting every phone conversation we have with that."

~

I don't often tell dad jokes.

But when I do, he usually laughs.

~

My friends surprised me with a massage for my bachelor party today.

I was really touched.

~

I've got a friend who has a butler, whose left arm is missing; serves him right.

~

I was at my girlfriend's house the other night, but her dad wouldn't let us sleep in the same bed.

Which was a shame, as he was pretty handsome.

~

I told my son that wetting your pants is nothing to be ashamed of.

It didn't work; he's still teasing me for it.

~

"Son, if you don't stop masturbating, you're going to go blind."

"Dad, I'm over here."

~

Wanna know the last thing my grandpa said before he kicked the bucket?

"I wonder how far I can kick this bucket."

~

My friend said to me: "What rhymes with orange?"

I said: "No it doesn't."

~

I'm going to donate my body to science, and keep my dad happy.

He always wanted me to go to medical school.

~

What's the difference between in-laws and outlaws?

Outlaws are wanted.

~

My father convinced me to donate my organs after I die.

He's a man after my own heart.

~

As a child, I was made to walk the plank.

We couldn't afford a dog.

~

My friend said that his alarm clock won't stop going off.

I said, "Well that's alarming."

~

About a month before my grandfather died, we covered his back with lard.

After that, he went downhill very quickly.

~

My brother just admitted that he broke my favorite lamp.

I'm not sure I'll be able to look at him in the same light ever again.

~

People say using your children's names as passwords isn't secure, but I don't agree, and nor do my kids, Ben_42! and Jenna123?.

~

My friend told me she loves the smell of books.

I said, "Just to be clear, you do know how reading works right?"

~

I have an EpiPen.

My friend gave it to me when he was dying, it seemed very important to him that I have it.

~

Don't vaccinate your kids!

Have a doctor do it instead.

~

My dad always said: "The first rule of theater is to always leave them wanting more."

He was a great actor. Bad anesthesiologist though.

~

My best friend loved tractors but one day he fell off a tractor, broke his leg and never rode one again.

Two years later I had a night out with him and he invited me back to his house. Upon arriving we noticed that his house was full of smoke! To my surprise, he took in a deep breath and blew all the smoke out in one exhale.

"How the hell did you do that?!" I asked him.

"I'm an ex-tractor fan."

~

My mate texted me and asked what I was doing.

"Probably failing my driving test," I replied.

~

My brother fell into an upholstery machine.

It's okay. He's completely recovered.

~

Friend: "You know change is inedible."

Me: "Don't you mean inevitable?"

Friend (Coughing out coins): "Nope, inedible."

~

My sister asked me to take off her clothes.

So I took off her shirt. Then she said, "Now take off my skirt." I took off her skirt. "Now my shoes." I took off her shoes. "Now take off my bra and panties." and so I took them off.

Then she looked at me and said, "I don't want to catch you wearing my things ever again."

~

I would like to thank my father for driving me to my wedding.

Without him, I wouldn't be here today.

~

My daughter asked for a Cinderella themed birthday party.

So I made her and her friends mop the floor and do the dishes.

~

My dad´s always complaining about the cost of things.

"$4.50 for a coffee? $9.75 for a miserable ham sandwich?" Honestly, he was moaning about it all afternoon. That´s the last time I invite him over to my house.

~ ~ ~

LOVE & MARRIAGE

I noticed a gorgeous woman in a green dress, but she wasn't interested.

My green dress probably put her off.

~

I went to a really emotional wedding the other day.

Even the cake was in tiers.

~

Two antennas met on a roof, fell in love and got married.

The ceremony wasn't great, but the reception was excellent.

~

Never marry a tennis player.

Love means nothing to them.

~

On our honeymoon, my new wife told me I was an awful lover.

I don't know how she could determine that in just 2 minutes.

~

My secretary reminds me of my wife.

I was unbuttoning her blouse at lunch today and she said, "Remember you have a wife."

~

"How is your long distance relationship going?"

"So far, so good."

~

Why are Mathematicians always single?

Because they can't stop talking about an x.

~

You only need 2.5 inches to pleasure a woman.

Doesn't matter if it's Visa or Mastercard.

~

My wife and I go out for a romantic meal twice a week.

She goes on Thursdays, I go on Saturdays.

~

I came home from work to see a note on the refrigerator: "I'm leaving you, and I'm taking the kids."

So I quickly pulled the plug out...you're not going anywhere my friend!

~

My wife and I decided not to have kids.

The kids are taking it pretty hard.

~

My wife is turning 32 soon.

I've told her not to get her hopes up for her birthday. "After all," I said, "The celebrations are only going to last half a minute."

"What are you talking about?" she asked.

"What? It's your thirty-second birthday isn't it?"

~

"What does the word 'gay' mean?" asked a son to his father.

"It means 'happy'", replied the father.

"Oh," contested the son, "So are you gay then?"

"No son, I have a wife."

~

I got my wife a "Get well soon" card.

I hope she does or we'll dehydrate.

~

After making love the woman turns to the man and says, "You know, I used to be Christian."

The man said, "It's all right, I don't really care for those sorts of things."

The woman replied, "Oh thank god! Life is so much better now that I'm Christine!"

~

A woman was telling me about her sexual attraction to beaches the other day.

Apparently, it comes in waves.

~

My wife says I'm stupid and uncultured, so to prove her wrong, guess where I'm taking her?

Hint: It starts with 'B' and rhymes with 'wallet'.

~

I invited my new boyfriend to go to the gym with me, but he stood me up.

I guess the two of us aren't going to work out.

~

I ended a long-term relationship today.

I'm not too bothered, it wasn't mine.

~

My wife told me that I twist everything she says to my advantage.

I took it as a compliment.

~

A man, shocked by how his buddy is dressed, asks him, "How long have you been wearing that bra?"

The friend replies, "Ever since my wife found it in the glove compartment."

~

I'm going to divorce my controlling wife...

when she lets me anyway.

~

My marriage ended recently.

I loved my wife Lorraine in the beginning, but I've always had a crush on my friend Claire-Lee Robins, who I know feels the same way about me. Eventually, Lorraine found out about my secretive feelings for her, and just like that, she packed her bags and left.

I do feel bad about it all. But then I realized; I can see Claire-Lee now Lorraine has gone.

~

Four guys are hanging out. One of them says, "Hey, did you know 1 out of every 4 guys is gay?"

One of the guys says, "I hope it's Chuck because he's really cute."

~

My girlfriend's a big fan of role-playing.

For the past five years, she's been playing my ex-girlfriend.

~

A therapist has a theory that couples who make love once a day are the happiest. So he tests it at a seminar by asking those assembled, "How many people here make love once a day?" Half the people raise their hands, each of them grinning widely. "Once a week?" A third of the audience raises their hand, their grins a bit less vibrant. "Once a month?" A few hands tepidly go up.

Then he asks, "OK, how about once a year?"

One man in the back jumps up and down, jubilantly waving his hands. The therapist is shocked - this disproves his theory.

"If you make love only once a year," he asks, "Why are you so happy?"

The man yells, "Today's the day!"

~

My wife was in labor with our first child when suddenly she began to shout, "Shouldn't, couldn't, wouldn't, didn't, can't!"

"Doctor, what's wrong with my wife?" I asked.

"Nothing," he said. "She's just having contractions."

~

A man eating in a restaurant is checking out a gorgeous redhead. Suddenly she sneezes and her glass eye comes flying out of its socket. The man reaches up, snatches it out of the air, and hands it back to her.

"I am so embarrassed," the woman says. "Would you like to join me for dinner?"

The man agrees and they enjoy a wonderful meal together. When they're finished, she invites him to the theater, followed by drinks. She pays for everything. Then she asks him to her place for a nightcap, and to stay for breakfast.

The next morning the guy is amazed. "Are you this nice to every guy you meet?" he asks.

"Not usually," she replies. "But you just happened to catch my eye."

~

At the maternity ward a new father, worried, asks the midwife, "Do you think my son looks like me?"

"Yes, but don't worry, the important thing is that he's healthy."

~

My wife left me because she said I was too condescending.

I doubt she even knows what that means.

~

My ex used to hit me with stringed instruments.

If only I had known about her history of violins.

~

Women really know how to hold a grudge over the smallest things.

The other day my wife asked me to pass her the lip balm, and by mistake, I gave her a tube of Super Glue.

It's been a month now and she's still not speaking to me.

~

I've fallen in love with a pencil and we're getting married!

I can't wait to introduce my parents to my bride 2B!

~

My girlfriend tried to persuade me to have sex with her on the hood of her Honda Civic.

I refused. If I'm going to have sex with her, it's going to be on my own Accord.

~

I've been waiting for this girl I like to make the first move.

I'm really nervous but my friend said to me, "Don't worry Jim, it's only a game of chess."

~

One of the things I look for in a girl is a love for pasta…

because eating pasta by yourself can get cannelloni.

~

My wife said I'm the cheapest person she's ever met.

I'm not buying it.

~

My wife came back from her holiday with the girls.

"How have you been?" she asked.

"I spent a week in bed with flu."

"Oh, that sounds terrible." she replied.

"Actually, that's not right, her name was Flo."

~

I've wanted to have a baby for about four years...

but my wife wants one forever.

~

"You're so childish!" screamed the wife, "Why do you always have to use that stupid walkie talkie?! This relationship is over!"

"This relationship is what? Over!"

~

My wife told me, 'Sex is better on holiday.'

That wasn't a very nice postcard to receive.

~

The lesbian couple upstairs got me a new Rolex for Christmas.

I think they may have misunderstood when I told them I wanna watch.

~

Just got a girl's number...

nine more and I'll have her full phone number.

~

My girlfriend accused me of cheating the other day.

I told her she was starting to sound like my wife.

~

My wife and I were happy for about 20 years...

and then we met.

~

I used to go out with an anesthetist - she was a local girl.

~

My wife got angry when I said her new candle smells like wet dog and mildew.

I was just giving my two scents on the topic.

~

I used to live in a flat with three girls...

until they found out.

~

My wife had a tantrum while we were playing scrabble and she threw a G at me, then an N, then a B, and then an A.

I said, "Hey, that's bang out of order!"

~

A wife asked her husband, "Dear, do you prefer a pretty woman or an intelligent woman?"

The husband then replied, "Neither, my love, I prefer you."

~

My wife and I were sitting at a table at her high school reunion. She kept staring at a drunken man swigging a beer as he sat at a nearby table.

I asked her, "Do you know him?"

"Yes," she sighed, "He's my old boyfriend. I understand he took to drinking right after we split up those many years ago and he hasn't been sober since."

"Wow," I said, "Who would think a person could go on celebrating for so long!"

~

I'm not saying my wife's a bad cook...

but she uses the smoke alarm as a timer.

~

My ex-wife still misses me...

but her aim is getting better.

~

My wife had a go at me for throwing a snowball at my son.

I'm also permanently banned from the maternity ward.

~

I told my wife she'd painted her eyebrows a little too high this morning.

She seemed surprised.

~

I finally approached my hot coworker and told her how I felt!

Turns out she felt the same way, so I turned on the air conditioning.

~

I like to cook for my husband after sex.

He has always liked coming home from work to a hot meal.

~

My wife said that our son feels neglected.

I said, "Who?"

~

What do you call the wife of a hippie?

Mississippi.

~

Is my wife dissatisfied with my body?

A small part of me says yes.

~

My wife asked me the other day: "Are you even listening to me?"

Which is a really weird way to start a conversation if you ask me.

~

My wife accused me of being immature.

I told her to get out of my fort.

~

A boy in my class asked a girl out and got a girlfriend.

I asked a girl out in my class and I lost my teacher's license.

~

I think my wife is secretly a weather forecaster...

a guy just called up asking if the coast was clear.

~

"Honey, I took your advice and got a new hair color, what do you think?"

"I think you misunderstood what I meant when I said it's time to diet."

~

My wife is divorcing me because I'm obsessed with Football coaching.

In my defense, I have J.J.Watt, Michael Bennett, and Richard Sherman.

~

Sex therapists claim that the most effective way to arouse a man is to lick his ear for 10 minutes.

Personally, I think it's nuts.

~

My wife kicked me out of the house because my Arnold Schwarzenegger impression was really bad.

But don't worry...I'll return.

~ ~ ~

ANIMALS

I'm reading a book about an immortal dog.

It's impossible to put down.

~

I gifted my friend an elephant ornament to put in his bedroom.

He said, "Thanks."

I said, "Don't mention it."

~

My girlfriend told me to take a spider out instead of killing it.

We went out and had some drinks. Cool guy, wants to be a lawyer.

~

I love eBay...

sold my homing pigeon eight times last month.

~

A friend of mine tried to annoy me with bird puns,
but I soon realized that toucan play at that game.

~

Why do dogs always race to the door when the
doorbell rings?

It's hardly ever for them.

~

I once had a goldfish who could break dance on the
carpet...

but he could only do it for 20 seconds...and only
once.

~

Sometimes I like to sit my dog down for a
performance review, just to remind him who's boss.

~

My friend and I were watching my dog lick his balls when he said, "I sure wish I could do that!"

I said, "You can try but I don't think he'll let you."

~

You would think that taking off a snail's shell would make it move faster...

but it actually makes it more sluggish.

~

My dog used to chase people on a bike.

It got so bad that eventually, I had to take his bike away.

~

I hide photos on my computer of me petting other animals in a folder named 'Fireworks and Vacuums'.

Just so my dog won't find them.

~

I was going to tell you the joke about my imaginary cat, but I'm not feeling it.

~

My dog just licked the crumbs out of my computer keyboard and earned an online college degree.

~

Generally speaking, I think it's fair to say that I am a friend to the creatures of the earth...

when I'm not eating them or wearing them anyway.

~

What do you call a parade of rabbits hopping backward?

A receding hare-line.

~

My dog named Minton ate my shuttlecock...

Bad Minton!

~

Why did the sick falcon get deported?

It was an ill eagle.

~

Which side of a duck has the most feathers?

The outside.

~

What do you call an elephant that doesn't matter?

Irrelephant.

~

Give a man a fish and you'll feed him for a day.

But teach him to fish and you'll save yourself a fish.

~

My doctor thinks I've been hallucinating. How do I know?

Let's just say a little bird told me.

~

My girlfriend's dog died, so to cheer her up I went out and got her an identical one.

She was livid: "What am I going to do with two dead dogs?"

~

"Lovely bonfire John! How did you get these baked potatoes to taste so meaty?"

"They're hedgehogs."

~

Two cows are talking in a field, when the first cow says, "Hey man, you worried about this mad cow disease that is going around?"

The second cow says, "Yeah, but I'm glad it doesn't affect us helicopters."

~

How many flies does it take to screw in a light bulb?

Two, but I don't know how they get in there.

~

I went to a zoo the other day but the only animal there was a dog.

It was a Shih Tzu.

~

"Race you home!" said the tortoise.

The hare began sprinting.

The tortoise retracted into his shell.

~

The star attraction at my local aquarium has been repossessed.

Turns out it was a loan shark.

~

I was watching a marathon the other day and saw one runner dressed as a chicken and another as an egg.

I thought, well this could be interesting.

~ ~ ~

FOOD & DRINK

Do you think oranges become juice willingly?

Or are they getting pressured into it?

~

I've started telling everyone about the benefits of eating dried grapes.

It's all about raisin awareness.

~

My wife gets upset every time I steal her kitchen utensils...

but it's a whisk I'm willing to take.

~

Why did the cranberry sauce cross the road?

To get to the other sides.

~

I used to be a world champion marathon runner but I gave it up when frozen eggs started competing.

They were just impossible to beat.

~

If you think alcohol is a solution you need help.

It's a solvent.

~

I got to insult an espresso yesterday.

It was a really good roast.

~

I made a chicken caesar salad today.

Stupid thing won't even eat it.

~

I put my root beer in a square glass.

Now it's just beer.

~

I had a gluten-free, lactose-free, low-carb pizza for dinner tonight.

It was a raw tomato.

~

I have an impressive collection of vintage kitchen utensils but there's one which I'm not sure what the intended purpose of it is. It looks like a cross between a metal slotted spoon and a spatula, so I use it as both. When not in use, it is prominently displayed in a decorative ceramic utensil caddy in my kitchen.

The mystery of the spoon/spatula was recently solved when I found one in its original packaging at a rummage sale.

It's a pooper-scooper.

~

I had to clean out my spice rack and found everything was too old and had to be thrown out.

What a waste of thyme.

~

I once ate a watch.

It was time consuming.

~

A Spanish man went to a restaurant right next to a bullfighting arena.

He always ordered the same thing after a bullfight, 2 bull testicles cooked to perfection. The man did this every week for months and was always satisfied with the taste and the size of the bull testicles until one week he was disappointed with the size and taste of the testicles. Confused, he decided to ask his waiter why this was.

The waiter replies, "But Señor, the Matador does not always win."

~

I trapped a couple of vegans in my basement.

Well, at least I think they're vegans. They keep shouting "Lettuce Leaf!"

~

I just got a free meal at Pizza Hut!

Apparently, they do it for everyone who jumps out of the toilet window and runs away.

~

I was preparing a bowl of cereal, finished 1 box of raisin bran and started another to fill my bowl. I was surprised when I saw a different colored cereal.

Then I realized they were different brans.

~

A hot blonde orders a double entendre at the bar.

The bartender gave it to her.

~

What's the difference between a pizza and a musician?

A pizza can feed a family of four.

~

My three favorite things are eating my family and not using commas.

~

A vegan told me: "People who sell meat are disgusting."

I said: "People who sell fruits and vegetables are grocer."

~

I think the Rainforest Cafe takes the whole rainforest theme too far.

This one time I was sitting there eating my meal and they bulldozed 40% of the restaurant.

~

Waiter: I see your glass is empty, would you like another one?

Me: Why would I want two empty glasses?

~

A man just threw some milk, cream, and butter at me...

how dairy!

~

What do you get after eating too much alphabet soup?

A large vowel movement.

~

You say I only eat toast, but I say I get three square meals a day.

~ ~ ~

DAILY LIFE

I was going to nail a shelf to my wall, but then I thought...

screw it!

~

When I was a single man, I had plenty of free time.

Now that I listen to full albums, I hardly ever leave the house.

~

Yesterday, a clown held the door open for me.

It was such a nice jester!

~

I'm reading a horror story in Braille at the moment. Something bad is gonna happen...

I can feel it.

~

People hate me for buying a record player...

but I think it was a sound investment.

~

My email account got hacked again.

That's the third time I've had to rename my cat.

~

These essential oils are terrible.

I've drank three bottles now and all they've done is give me a headache and diarrhea.

~

I used to attend a book club at my local church but I stopped going as we kept re-reading the same book.

~

I'm not saying I haven't achieved much in life but some of my proudest moments have been when a website has told me my password was "Very Strong".

~

I have a phobia of speed bumps, but I'm slowly getting over it.

~

I thought I'd try Viagra to see if I could benefit from them so I went to my local chemist thinking I may need a prescription.

"Can I get it over the counter?" I asked the assistant.

"You might if you take two."

~

At first, I didn't like the idea of having a beard...

but it's starting to grow on me.

~

I used to really enjoy political jokes...

unfortunately, too many of them got elected.

~

Autocorrect always makes me say things I didn't Nintendo.

~

So after winning the game, I decided to throw the ball into the crowd like they do on TV.

Apparently, this is unacceptable in bowling.

~

Just read a review of Orion's Belt.

Three stars.

~

I had my first appointment with the psychiatrist today.

He thinks I'm paranoid.

He didn't say it, but I knew he was thinking it.

~

Spelling can be hard.

You mix up two letters and your whole joke is urined.

~

We can argue all day about what the best card game is but I think we can all agree...

Uno is number 1.

~

I was going to tell you the joke about my favorite maritime board game but it's a bit hit and miss.

~

The inventor of the USB drive was lowered into his grave.

Then lifted back up, flipped over, and laid in again.

~

Nothing is built in America these days...

I just bought a T.V. and it says "built in antenna".

~

Last night I was at the bar when the waitress screamed, "Anyone know CPR!?"

I said, "Hell yeah, I know the entire alphabet!"

~

What starts with 'P', ends with 'orn', and is popular in the film industry?

Popcorn.

~

I needed a password with 8 characters.

In the end, I used "Snow White and the Seven Dwarves".

~

I don't want any other races in my neighborhood.

There's already a marathon in July and it makes getting home a nightmare.

~

I started reading a report about Satan the other day, but they don't even mention him in the executive summary.

I guess the devil's in the detail.

~

I'm no longer a 19-year-old loser!

I turned 20 today.

~

So apparently shops are now selling tampons with bells on.

Probably just for the Christmas period.

~

My printer kept playing random music so I decided to call support.

"Don't worry," they said, "It's just the paper jamming."

~

Last week I called someone a watering hole but I meant well.

~

I was caught peeing in the local swimming pool.

The lifeguard yelled at me so loudly, I nearly fell in.

~

I bought a book about the dangers of deforestation.

The first page says: "You're not helping!"

~

Today a man knocked on my door and asked for a small donation to the local swimming pool.

So I gave him a glass of water.

~

I went to the shop to buy 6 cans of Sprite.

It's only when I got home that I realized I had picked 7 up.

~

I gave blood today.

I really hate all those personal questions they ask.

Like "Whose blood is this?" and "Where did you get it?"

~

Today, I gave my phone, my watch, and $500 to a homeless man. Words cannot describe how happy I felt...

when he put his gun away.

~

I wonder why the person who invented the week decided to make it seven days long.

It's such an odd number.

~

There was a streaker at church this week.

It took some time but they eventually caught him by the organ.

~ ~ ~

A MAN WALKS INTO A BAR...

A pun, a play on words, and a limerick walk into a bar.

No joke.

~

Helvetica and Times New Roman walk into a bar.

"Get out of here!" shouts the bartender, "We don't serve your type!"

~

A man walks into a bar and sees a large girl dancing on a table. He walks over to her and says, "Wow, nice legs!"

She is flattered and replies, "You really think so?"

The man says, "Oh definitely! Most tables would have collapsed by now!"

~

A Roman walks into a bar, holds up two fingers and says...

"Five beers, please."

~

A man walks into a bar.

He sits down at the counter and the bowl of peanuts next to him says, "Looking good today sir!"

The guy turns to the bartender and says, "Whoa, what's up with those peanuts?"

The bartender says, "They're complimentary!"

~

Three conspiracy theorists walk into a bar...

you can't tell me that's just a coincidence...

~

A bear walks into a bar.

The bear says, "I'd like a whiskey and............................coke please."

The bartender says, "Why the big pause?"

The bear replies, "I was born with them."

~

A guy walks into a bar and asks, "What's the WiFi password?"

Bartender: "You need to buy a drink first."

Guy: "Okay, I'll have a coke."

Bartender: "Is Pepsi okay?"

Guy: "Sure, How much is that?"

Bartender: "£3."

Guy: "There you go. So what's the wifi password?"

Bartender: "You need to buy a drink first. No spaces, all lowercase."

~ ~ ~

CRIME & PUNISHMENT

Police station broken into, toilets stolen.

Cops have nothing to go on.

~

The world tongue-twister champion just got arrested.

I hear they're gonna give him a really tough sentence.

~

One time I saw a kid getting bullied by 4 kids, so I decided to step in...

he didn't stand a chance against all 5 of us.

~

I just purchased some shoes from a drug dealer.

I don't know what he laced them with but I've been tripping all day.

~

If you advertise your big new TV by putting the box out in the trash, I'm gonna steal it.

My cardboard fort only needs a few more pieces.

~

Why do mathematicians have the lowest murder rate?

There's safety in numbers.

~

A criminal set up a small souvenir shop in Australia selling glass Kangaroos as a front for his drug smuggling business.

The detective working the case walks in and says, "I can see straight through your roos mate."

~

A detective was interviewing the victim of an assault.

The victim described the assailant as a leather box with a handle on it. The culprit was arrested 30 minutes later.

It was a brief case.

~

A woman shoots her husband

The police officer jumps into his squad car and calls the station.

"I have an interesting case here," he says, "A woman just shot her husband for stepping on the floor she just mopped."

"Have you arrested her?" asked the sergeant.

"No not yet, the floor is still wet."

~

I came home from work today to find someone had broken in and stolen my limbo stick.

I mean, how low can you go?

~

Why did the baby get in trouble with the police for not napping?

She was resisting a rest.

~

I hate people who take drugs.

Especially border security.

~

Officer: "Where did the hackers go?"

"Not sure, they just ransomware."

~

My drug dealer is so funny, he really cracks me up.

~

The FBI just arrested a math teacher holding some graph paper.

He was definitely plotting something.

~

Why was the CEO of a leading prosthetics company arrested?

It came out that he was involved in international arms dealing.

~

A drug dealer asked me if I wanted some cannabis and I said, "Yes please." He then asked if I wanted some heroin and I said, "Yes please." He then offered me some cocaine.

And I said, "No thanks, coke is where I draw the line."

~

Three old ladies were sitting on a park bench when a man in a trench-coat walks by and flashes them. Two of the old ladies had a stroke.

The other one couldn't reach that far.

~

My friend and I were talking the other day and he asked me: "So why did your dad go to prison then?"

I said, "Beats me."

~

My grandma told me her joints are getting weaker, so I told her to roll them tighter.

~ ~ ~

MISCELLANEOUS

I don't trust stairs...

they're always up to something.

~

Communism was bound to fail.

There were a lot of red flags.

~

I just started practicing some speed reading techniques. Last night I read "War and Peace" in about 40 seconds.

I know it's only 3 words but it's a start!

~

I read every synonym out loud today...

gave me thesaurus throat ever!

~

That's it; I've had enough of abbreviations...

and everything they stand for!

~

What's the best thing about Switzerland?

I don't know, but their flag is a huge plus.

~

Why aren't people in Afghanistan allowed to watch TV?

Because of the telly ban.

~

What happens when you cross a joke with a rhetorical question?

~

Doctor Frankenstein entered a bodybuilding competition...

but vastly misunderstood the objective.

~

Two men are stranded on a boat with three cigarettes but nothing to light them with.

One man throws a cigarette overboard, and the whole boat becomes a cigarette lighter.

~

Sign up today for a new 24 letter alphabet!

No BS.

~

I found a Kanye West concert ticket nailed to a tree, so I took it.

You never know when you might need a nail.

~

I don't think I need a spine...

It's holding me back.

~

What's the leading cause of dry skin?

Towels.

~

Whoever invented the knock-knock joke really deserves a No-bell Prize.

~

My new hairdryer is so strong.

It's mind-blowing.

~

I was asked to describe myself in just three words.

I said, "Lazy."

~

I like to play chess with bald men in the park.

Although it's usually quite hard to find 32 of them.

~

The Low Self Esteem Support Group will meet on Thursday at 7 PM.

The entrance is at the rear of the building.

~

What is the least spoken language in the world?

Sign language.

~

What do cheap hotels and designer jeans have in common?

No ballroom.

~

You Matter.

Unless you are multiplied by the speed of light squared; then you energy.

~

When people began using the alphabet, they only used 25 letters.

Nobody knew why.

~

What starts and ends with "e" and only contains one letter?

An envelope.

~

Have you heard of the comedian who's a giant hand dryer?

He's a big fan of dry humor.

~

The boating store was having a big sale on canoes.

It was quite the oar deal.

~

Correct punctuation: the difference between a sentence that's well-written and a sentence that's, well, written.

~

I bought a new thesaurus today.

It's nothing to write house about.

~

I hate Russian Nesting Dolls.

They're so full of themselves.

~

Apparently, Donald Trump is going to ban the production of string cheese.

I guess he wants to make America grate again.

~

What do you mean, I didn't win? I ate more wet T-shirts than anyone else.

~

I just found the worst page in the entire dictionary.

What I saw was disgraceful, disgusting, dishonest, and disingenuous.

~

I once entered a pun contest. I sent in ten different puns, in the hope that at least one of the puns would win.

No pun in ten did.

~

I can't believe the National Spelling Bee ended in a tye.

~

Initially, I wasn't going to get a brain transplant, but then I changed my mind.

~

I was going to make myself a belt made out of watches the other day, but then I realized it would be a waist of time.

~

Seriously, what are Roman numerals actually good IV?

~

I just invented a new word - Plagiarism!

~

As soon as the hospital made me put on one of those silly gowns, I knew the end was in sight.

~

If you obsess too much, you have OCD.

If you eat too much, you have OBCD.

~

Can February March?

No, but April May.

~

Did you hear about the fight between nineteen and twenty?

Twenty-one.

~

I'm against picketing, but I don't know how to show it.

~

I don't hate lazy people anymore.

I've found someone else to do it for me.

~

What word becomes shorter when you add two letters to it?

Short.

~

I was going to tell you my joke about blunt pencils, but it's a bit pointless.

~

During a visit to the mental asylum, I asked the director, "How do you determine whether or not a patient should be institutionalized?"

"Well," said the director, "We fill up a bathtub, and then we offer a teaspoon, a teacup and a bucket to the patient and ask them to empty the bathtub."

"Oh, I understand," I said, "A normal person would use the bucket because it's bigger than the spoon or the teacup."

"No," said the director, "A normal person would just pull the bathtub plug out. Do you want a bed near the window?"

~

Wanna hear a joke about sodium?

"Na."

~

I used to be terrible at telling jokes.

I always used to punch up the messline.

~

What gym do Christians visit to exercise?

Jehovah's Fitness.

~

My penis used to be in the Guinness book of world records...

until I was kicked out of the library.

~

Do you make grass slippery? Do you make windows wet? Are you a morning person?

If so, you may be dew condensation.

~

I published a book on camouflage recently.

You won't find it in the bookshops though.

~

I always laugh at jokes about regions with small mountains.

They're just hill-areas!

~

I hate people who don't know the difference between "your" and "you're".

There so stupid.

~

Breaking news: Vandals have just attacked the National Origami Museum in Tokyo.

We'll keep you updated as the story unfolds.

~

I started a club for erectile dysfunction sufferers.

It was a flop, nobody came.

~

The furniture store won't stop calling me!

All I wanted was one nightstand.

~

Wife: "Did you know the library has a telescope that you can borrow?"

Me: "Huh, we should look into that."

~

I saw an ad for burial plots and thought to myself, this is the last thing I need.

~

Want to prove you're dead when you pass away?

Get a will, it's a dead giveaway.

~

I cannot believe there's no cure for obesity yet.

I thought it would be a walk in the park.

~

A guy asked a girl in a university library: "Do you mind if I sit beside you?" The girl replied with a loud voice, "No, I don't want to spend the night with you!"

All the students in the library stared at the guy; he was truly embarrassed.

After a couple of minutes, the girl walked quietly to the guy's table and said, "I study psychology, and I know what a man is thinking. I guess you felt embarrassed, right?"

The guy then responded with a loud voice, "$500 for one night? That's way too much!"

All the people in the library looked at the girl in shock.

The guy stood up and whispered in her ear, "I study law; I know how to screw people."

~

"That's what she said," is a really versatile punchline to a joke because you can put it almost anywhere.

That's what she said.

~

What is the phobia of chainsaws called?

Common sense.

~

I went to the doctor's the other day.

I said, "I feel like a woman who delivers babies!"

"Don't worry," he said, "It's just a midwife crisis."

~

So there's this guy going around dipping his testicles in glitter.

It's pretty nuts.

~

I conducted a survey of 100 women to see which shampoo was the most popular.

The number one response was: How the hell did you get in here?

~

I did a book signing at the library the other day.

But I only managed to sign three books from the shelves before they asked me to leave.

~

I was late for my poker game the other day. When I arrived a man got up from the table, stripped naked, and ran around the room.

I guess he was on a winning streak.

~

To the people who hate hand gestures...

I salute you.

~

I was going to tell you my joke about bacterial disease, but I don't want to spread it.

~

What's the difference between a good and a bad joke timing.

~

How do you spot a blind man at a nude beach?

C'mon, it's not hard.

~

What's the difference between a well-dressed man on a bicycle and a poorly-dressed man on a unicycle?

Attire.

~

I've decided that from January 1st, I'm only going to watch things that are 1080p and above.

It's my new year's resolution.

~

I once met a soldier who had never lost a battle.

Turns out he'd never actually fought in a battle either.

~

I got a rejection letter from the origami university today.

I'm not sure what to make of it.

~

Parallel lines have so much in common.

It's a shame they'll never meet.

~

I stand corrected, said the man in the orthopedic shoes.

~

Why does Waldo wear stripes?

He doesn't want to be spotted.

~

A woman is sitting at her recently deceased husband's funeral. A man leans into her and asks, "Do you mind if I say a word?"

"No, go right ahead." the woman replies.

The man stands, clears his throat, and says "Plethora." He then sits back down.

"Thanks," the woman says, "That means a lot."

~

Did you hear about the man with 5 penises?

He went to the doctor and said, "Doc, I have five penises. I want to know what is wrong."

The doctor replied, "5 penises! How the hell do your pants fit?"

"Like a glove!" the man replied.

~

Where did Sally go during the bombing?

Everywhere.

~

If I go around spanking statues, does that mean I've hit rock bottom?

~

I just heard there's a nudist's convention next week.

I might go if I've got nothing on.

~

What do cars and Scientology have in common?

Cruise control.

~

Does anyone want my old copies of Chiropractor Monthly?

I've got loads of back issues.

~

Instead of a swear jar, I have a negativity jar. Every time I have pessimistic thoughts, I put a dollar in it.

It's currently half empty.

~

As I suspected, someone has been adding soil to my garden.

The plot thickens.

~

I was going to include my joke about blunt scissors in the book, but unfortunately it didn't make the cut.

~

Sometimes it is very important if a sentence was said by a man or a woman

A good example: "I used a whole pack of tissues during that awesome movie yesterday!"

~

I have managed to become a member of the National Secrecy Society.

I can't tell you how much this means to me.

~

I think I might have scoliosis. How do I know?

Let's just say, I have a hunch.

~ ~ ~

OBSERVATIONAL HUMOR

For some reason whenever I undress in my bathroom, my shower gets turned on.

~

You know you're getting old when you go to an antique auction and three people bid on you.

~

In Heaven, I hope you get back all the Chapsticks you lost.

~

If you can't beat them, arrange to have them beaten.

~

I bet cats have a secret website where they upload clips of cute humans trying to open DVD packaging and jump-start cars.

~

It's amazing how a person can compliment and insult you at the same time.

Recently, when I greeted my coworker, she said, "You look gorgeous today, I didn't even recognize you!"

~

If you stop eating doughnuts you will live three years longer, but it's just three more years that you'll want a doughnut.

~

Why is there an expiration date on sour cream?

~

How come you never see a headline like "Psychic Wins Lottery"?

~

Ever notice that anyone going slower than you is an idiot, but anyone going faster is a maniac?

~

Whoever said, "It's not whether you win or lose that counts" probably lost.

~

A synonym is just a word you use when you can't spell the first word you thought of.

~

Forgetting an email attachment is the 21st-century version of licking an envelope shut and then realizing you forgot to put the letter inside.

~

There are two types of people who drive at 4 am:

Those who need to get a job.

And those who need to get a different job.

~

Is anyone else as apprehensive about throwing out a shoe box as I am?

~

An ad for a hedge clipper that I had to read twice: "A built-in safety switch prevents accidental starting; blades will stop when you take one hand off."

~

Just before I die, I'm going to eat a whole bag of unpopped popcorn.

That should make the cremation a little more interesting.

~

Saying "My dog is a rescue." is just a self-righteous way of saying I bought a used dog.

~

I just saw a homeless man picking unfinished cigarettes up off the floor.

It's nice that he's doing his bit for the environment.

~

The cool part about naming your kids is that you don't have to add a bunch of random numbers if the name has already been taken.

~

Give a man a gun and he'll rob the bank.

Give a man a bank and he'll rob the world.

~

I feel like a lot of conflict in the Wild West could have been completely avoided...

if cowboy architects had just made their towns big enough for everyone.

~ ~ ~

Made in the USA
Monee, IL
15 December 2019